GOD in Me.
GOD in Everything.

Hannah Caudill

Trilogy Christian Publishers
A Wholly Owned Subsidary of Trinity Broadcasting Network
2442 Michelle Drive
Tustin, CA 92780

For information, address Trilogy Christian Publishing
Rights Department, 2442 Michelle Drive, Tustin, CA 92780.
Trilogy Christian Publishing/ TBN and colophon are trademarks of Trinity Broadcasting Network.

For information about special discounts for bulk purchases, please contact Trilogy Christian Publishing.

10 9 8 7 6 5 4 3 2 1

Library of Congress Cataloging-in-Publication Data is available.

ISBN 979-8-89041-550-9
ISBN 979-8-89041-551-6 (ebook)

Dedication

I dedicate this book foremost to my Lord and Savior, Jesus Christ. I am thankful for the companionship of His Holy Spirit that gave me the words and helped me move forward in having this book published. Also, to my family, Kevin, Taylor, and Sawyer, who prayed over this book and encouraged me to be a vessel for the Lord. I would also like to thank my sisters, Leigh-ana, Ashley, and Mandy, for praying that GOD's will be done!

He hung the sun,
He hung the moon.
He made them to rise, and
He made them to set.
My GOD is great!

My GOD's voice is in the quiet,
My GOD's voice is in the storm.
My GOD's voice can be found in everything.
My GOD is great!

I can find Him in the valley,
I can find Him on the mountain.
My GOD loves to be with me.
And I love to be with Him.
My GOD is great!

All good and perfect gifts come from Him.
He gave us His son.
I am thankful for Jesus and all that He has done.
My GOD is great!

He is my best friend.
He teaches me to share,
Showing me daily how much that He cares.
My GOD is great!

11

He is generous and kind,
He is strong, and He is brave,
He does what is right,
He can do no wrong.
My GOD is great!

My GOD is King!
He rules, and He reigns
Over both the heavens and the earth.
His name is higher than all others.
My GOD is great!

His splendor is unmatched,
Holy in all His ways.
He is clothed in glory, honor, and majesty.
My GOD is great!

17

He is awesome in power,
With unlimited wisdom,
An abundance of strength,
And infinite understanding.
My GOD is great!

19

The heavens cannot contain Him,
Nor can a house box Him in.
Time will not constrain Him.
My GOD is great!

My GOD is my shelter,
My hiding place.
I know that He is protecting me
In everything that I face.
My GOD is great!

23

I trust my GOD.

He never lies.

He will forever be with me,

Always by my side.

My GOD is great!

6'

5'10"

5'8"

5'6"

5'4"

5'2"

5'

4'10"

4'8"

4'6"

4'4"

4'2"

25

He is my encourager,
My peace, my joy, my hope.
I find everything I need in Him,
Everything I need to grow.
My GOD is great!

I am saved by grace,
Through faith in Jesus,
Trusting that He is leading me
Perfectly along the way.
My GOD is great.

Printed in the USA
CPSIA information can be obtained
at www.ICGtesting.com
CBHW051425030824
12613CB00071B/1282